House Beautiful

COLOR WORKSHOP

House Beautiful

COLOR WORKSHOP
DECORATING STYLISH ROOMS

SARAH CHILDS-CARLILE

HEARST BOOKS
A Division of Sterling Publishing Co., Inc.
New York

Created, edited, and designed by Duncan Baird Publishers Ltd., Castle House, 75–76 Wells Street, London W1T 3QH

Managing Editor: Emma Callery
Designer: Alison Shackleton

Library of Congress Cataloging-in-Publication Data Available.

1 2 3 4 5 6 7 8 9 10

Published by Hearst Books
A Division of Sterling Publishing Co., Inc.
387 Park Avenue South, New York, NY 10016

House Beautiful and Hearst Books are trademarks of Hearst Communications, Inc.

www.housebeautiful.com

For information about custom editions, special sales, premium, and corporate purchases, please contact Sterling Special Sales Department at 800-805-5489 or specialsales@sterlingpub.com.

Distributed in Canada by Sterling Publishing ℅ Canadian Manda Group, 165 Dufferin Street Toronto, Ontario, Canada M6K 3H6

Distributed in Australia by Capricorn Link (Australia) Pty. Ltd.
P.O. Box 704, Windsor, NSW 2756 Australia

Manufactured in China

ISBN 13: 978-1-58816-500-8
ISBN 10: 1-58816-500-0

CONTENTS

FOREWORD

Have you ever struggled to get the right color for a room or borrowed a color idea from somebody else's house only to feel it really didn't work in yours? We've all been there, and sometimes it is especially difficult to know exactly why it doesn't work, which is where *Color Workshop* comes into its own.

Whether we realize it or not, color has an enormous influence on the way a room looks, how we use it, and even how we feel when we're in it. You may get the feeling that a room is cold and unwelcoming just because of the color it's painted. Change the color and suddenly it becomes warm and inviting.

But let's face it, when it comes to starting from scratch, it's just so easy to use the same colors you always have. Or maybe you'll decide to strike out on a different course without really considering what will suit you, the room, and your lifestyle. Like clothing fashion, it's important to know what will suit a specific room, rather than slavishly following trends. Just as it's no good wearing fashionable purple if it doesn't make you look and feel great, it's no good painting a room in trendy neutrals if it happens to look dull and boring in that particular room.

In *Color Workshop*, we aim to help you address all these complex issues and get to know how to choose that perfect color for your own individual room. It may seem an overwhelming proposition at first, but it is actually pretty straightforward if you take it step by step.

The first thing to come to grips with is a rudimentary idea of how color works. Don't stop reading here if that sounds too technical! It's really very easy and will make an enormous difference to the success of your choices. Understanding the characteristics of individual colors, and, even more important, how they work together, is critical

and will probably make you far more adventurous in your choices than you might expect.

It's also very helpful to take a step-by-step planning approach, even when you think you have an inkling of the color scheme you might want. It's so tempting to rush out and buy everything you need to start painting, wallpapering, and hanging curtains, only to wake up one morning and realize it is far from your ideal. It may sound boring, but some hard work put in at the initial stages will pay huge dividends in the long run.

Once you have mastered the basics, you may find it quite easy to find the perfect solution for your rooms, but it has to be admitted that in an imperfect world, life is not always that straightforward. What happens if you have a really awkward room or space? Maybe your ceiling is too low or your corridors are too narrow. One of the things people find hardest to understand is that color really can help in these situations. It's amazing how different colors and the way in which they are used can "liberate" a room, hiding its defects and emphasizing its attributes.

Getting perfect color is not rocket science, but it is important to have a helping hand along the way. *Color Workshop* will provide you with just that and you'll find inspiration and friendly help from the text, the fabulous pictures, and the practical illustrations.

From the Editors of *House Beautiful*

COLOR
ESSENTIALS

COLOR COUNTS

Ever since man first daubed color on cave walls, we have been obsessed with stamping our own personality on our homes through the medium of color.

Those ancestors of ours were trying to represent the amazing natural world they saw around them, and the color we use in our home even now is heavily influenced by this. Just look around at the countless colors in the natural world and stand back in awe. It's hard to improve on the color combinations of a sunset, a moss rose, or even an artichoke.

Nature has had millions of years to get it right; you probably want to start right now. Taking nature as an inspiration, just as the cavemen did, is not such a bad idea, but with such an infinite choice of wonderful color used in nature, you need a bit more to go on.

▶ **Clever color**
The clever use of color can totally transform a room if you know how to make the most of it.

▼ **Be bold**
The adventurous colors used here lift this room far above the ordinary. A combination like this requires flair.

COLOR ESSENTIALS

The advantage we have over those early people is a far greater understanding of color. We now know how the colors we use in our homes can literally change the way we live. We know how to use different colors to create different moods, to change the proportions of rooms, and to harmonize the appearance of rooms with their use. We also have access to an overwhelmingly diverse palette of colors.

And how confusing does that make it all? How many times have you walked into a room and known that the color scheme works, or it doesn't, but you haven't known why? So if you want to make the most of your own rooms, you have to know how to use color, which is what this book is about. There is the initial groundwork to do, but once you understand the principles of color, you're set for a lifetime of creating wonderful interior schemes.

▲ Simple solution
The use of white with just touches of pattern and color makes this room simple and airy, but never bland.

▶ Grand designs
Bold stripes and an unusual combination of colors is a brave choice that works beautifully in this room, giving it a simple elegance and a touch of grandeur.

◀ Divide and rule
Some rooms serve more than one purpose, and it can be difficult to know how to decorate them. Here color has been used to divide different living areas and to bring warmth to a vast area.

HOW COLOR WORKS

primary

secondary

tints

shades

tone

complementary

harmonizing

accent

pattern

texture

THE COLOR WHEEL

Whether you have just moved to a new house or you are about to revamp the color scheme in your existing one, try to resist running for the paint cans and brushes. However tempting it may be to get started immediately, it pays to do a little color homework first.

Before you get anywhere near the overalls, you need an essential tool, and that is a color wheel. This is something you can buy from a store, and the illustration below is one such example. Knowledge of the color wheel is essential as this is where your understanding of color starts. It may look like a gimmick, but study it carefully and it will make your color choices far more successful and could also save you from making mistakes.

Look at the color wheel and you will see:
◆ **The primary colors**—red, blue, and yellow—are equally spaced around it.
◆ **The secondary colors** (those you get by mixing the two primary colors) lie halfway between the primaries. These are green, orange, and violet/purple.
◆ **Tertiary colors** lie between the primaries and the secondaries and are made by mixing the primary and secondary colors.

The color wheel is the basis of so many decisions, so make sure you keep referring back to it as you read the rest of the chapters. It gives a hands-on guide to how colors work together and why they sometimes don't!

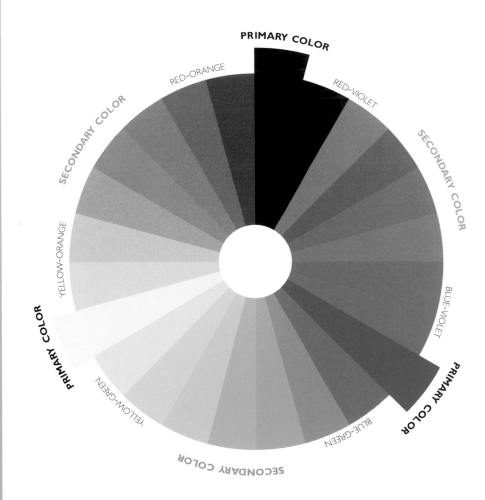

▶ Go-ahead red
Understanding how color works through using the color wheel will allow you to achieve success with bold colors, such as the stunning red used in this living room.

▶ Blues beater
This eye-catching blue could be disastrous in some rooms, but here it works well as a fitting backdrop to the grandeur of the mirror and the bookcases.

▶▶ Sunshine warmth
The light in this room is enhanced by the use of a warm custard yellow. It is also a few degrees removed from a primary yellow and suits the period overtones of the day bed and pictures.

TINTS & SHADES

The next step in understanding color is understanding tints and shades, which play an extremely important role in how effective a color is in a room.

The most important thing to remember is that:
◆ **Tints** range from a pure color to white. In other words, to experience the whole spectrum of tints, you just keep adding more and more white to a pure color.
◆ **Shades** is the term used for colors that range from a pure color to black. Add ever-increasing amounts of black to a pure color to get the whole spectrum.

This may not seem that important until you realize that using even subtly different tints and shades of the same color creates dramatic effects. For instance, in a monochrome scheme (shades and tints of one basic color), you can emphasize aspects of the room, or help others blend in until they almost disappear. You might use a paler tint to highlight an attractive feature, such as

a ceiling rose, or paint an ugly radiator the same color as the wall to make it fade into obscurity. Conversely, you could add depth to the room by painting a feature or range of features in a slightly deeper shade.

One more term that might be useful is tone:
◆ **Tone** is measured in terms of brightness. Look at a red and green room as a black and white photograph and the colors are almost indistinguishable because they have similar tones. Tone can be very important when it comes to combining colors; it can be more effective than color contrast.

▶ **Gentle tints**
The gentler tints of yellow and orange used in this room include buttermilk and apricot, and they introduce a soft gentleness that is wonderfully peaceful.

▲ **Sense of tone**
Think of a room where there are swathes of violet and some yellow. The yellow will dominate here because it is a brighter tone, even though violet and yellow are complementary colors (see page 20). In a black-and-white photo, the yellow will stand out far less and will appear as

the same shade of gray as the violet. You can use this to your advantage by remembering that brighter tones will dominate. However, if you use them cleverly, the combination can enhance both colors. Sunshine yellow against violet will make the yellow seem even "happier" and the violet more intensely restful.

COLOR COMBINATIONS

With the color wheel by your side, you can see at a glance which colors enhance each other.

◆ **Complementary—or contrasting—**colors are on opposite sides of the wheel (like violet and yellow) and make excellent combinations.

◆ **Harmonizing** colors sit next to or near each other on the wheel, such as yellow and orange, and yellow and green, and can be combined to very different effect.

The fun really starts here as you can begin to use color to create effects. As a general rule of thumb, harmonious colors look easy and natural together because they are closely related. For peaceful color schemes, use harmonious colors. You may be surprised at some of the seemingly strange bedfellows you find, such as red and pink, when you look at the wheel, but go with the theory and you'll find they do work in interiors.

For more dramatic effects, try complementary colors. Red and green are on opposite sides of the color wheel and look stunning when combined, but they will provide an eye-catching effect rather than a peaceful one. Unless you are used to life on the edge, it may be easier to choose your color contrasts from among the secondary and tertiary colors rather than the primaries as these are very vivid and can be difficult to live with.

If you look at the pairs of complementary colors on the wheel, such as blue and orange, one is always a warm color and the other a cool color. In color harmonies, the colors are all warm or all cool.

Sometimes, though, colors that seem similar, such as orange and pink-mauve, are actually different "temperatures," and when put together create a color shock. These can be more difficult to cope with unless you get exactly the right combination, but don't be over-timid as they can look absolutely stunning.

▶ **Sophisticated couple**
The complementary colors of blue and yellow have been used to enhance the cool sophistication of the icy blue, and to make the warm yellow seem more sunshiny.

COLOR ACCENTS

Try to think of an accent as a highlight color. It's really a small amount of color used to give a bit of a zing to an interior. Imagine it as a touch of spice added to a dish to lift it above the mundane.

Of course, as always with color, the combination is the all-important thing. Accent colors can be used in complementary or harmonizing schemes, but don't be fooled, the accent color will be just as important as the dominant color because it's all about the interaction between the two.

When you use two complementary colors, such as violet and yellow, the success of the look will depend on proportion. Equal amounts of complementary colors can be really tiring for your eyes to process, and your wonderful color scheme can lose its impact. Think of a room with equal amounts of violet and yellow and you may feel a headache creeping on, but vary the proportion and use a much smaller amount of either as an accent and suddenly the whole scheme is easier on the eye. Either can be the accent color, depending on what look you want to achieve.

Don't forget that you can also use accents with white to prevent a room from looking too sterile.

▶ Pistachio punctuation

Pistachio green cushions have been used repetitively as small blocks of accent color that lift the whole atmosphere of the room.

▲ Fine accent

White rooms can sometimes look a little bland, but small touches of accent color, such as the lime green coffee machine and ice bucket, will bring interest and warmth.

▲ Dashing red

This blue-and-white room is rescued from being boring and ordinary by adding two dashes of accent tomato red—a rug and an invitingly cozy throw.

TWO COLORS & BEYOND

So, color wheel firmly in hand, you are now ready to start experimenting with combining colors. Remember that complementary colors are opposites on the wheel and harmonizing colors are next or near to each other.

Color contrasts often work best with the use of just two colors, although others can be added. If you find, though, that there is just too much contrast, try adding a neutral or a white to balance the whole scheme.

For harmonies, you can afford to be a little more liberal and maybe combine three or even four closely related colors. As long as they are of similar hues, the scheme will work without one color dominating.

Keep in mind, too, that combinations can change the nature of the original color. For instance, primrose yellow on its own looks fresh, but combine it with black, and the yellow will appear quite harsh. Combine the same yellow with red and it will become much warmer. This is why it is always really important to test all your colors together before you commit yourself.

But what if you want to be a bit more adventurous? What if you want a multicolor effect? If that's the case, try to use colors that have similar tonal values. Remember tone is a measure of brightness, so a range of sorbet colors would sit very happily together.

▶▲ Balanced intensity

More than two colors have been successfully combined in this room, but because there are several intense colors, none dominates too much.

▶ Light touch

A light hand has brought together at least five different colors here, and the restraint with which they have been used makes the whole scheme work.

▶▶ Stunning couple

Complementary colors red and green have been combined to stunning effect, which is saved from extreme intensity by the neutral cream on the floor and ceiling.

PATTERN

So far we have been thinking about blocks of color, which can be relied upon to work in an ordered fashion. However, when pattern comes into play, some of the rules bend. Pattern combined with color can be the most incredible tool, but it's very easy to get it wrong. We've all been in rooms where the pattern is overdone, but never fear, there are some secrets that will help you use pattern to wonderful effect.

Pattern effects

◆ **As a rule of thumb,** look for patterns that focus on two main colors and two supporting ones as accents.

◆ **Don't be afraid** to mix together certain geometric patterns such as stripes and checks, or to mix different types of patterns, such as spots and florals. It is better to keep the same base color, to prevent a muddled or disjointed look.

◆ Remember to take all the colors in a pattern into account, not just the one that covers the biggest area. There may be quite small amounts of a very bright tone in your pattern, and they could end up taking center stage, which may not have been your intention.

◆ Pattern can change all the colors involved and create an unexpected effect. Add some cream-and-red striped curtains to your cozy, deep red dining room, and you will be creating blocks of pink not red; from a distance the cream and red will merge to create the effect of pink.

◆ Checkerboard patterns or diamonds on a floor can make a room look bigger, which is why they are often used in hallways.

▲ **Mix and match**
When using more than one pattern, take care. Mix patterns of roughly the same size as shown here and make sure that none is too dominant a color.

▲ **Winning checkers**
A careful use of pattern can work in your favor. For example, a checkerboard design can make even a small area of floor look much larger.

▶ **Balancing act**
Although this room uses several different patterns, they have been cleverly balanced by repeating the same intensity of color.

FINISHES

When you are working with color, one of the things that is easy to forget is how different textures and finishes can change the final effect. Think of the same color in different finishes. Imagine a shiny glazed vase in navy blue and then imagine the same color in a matte cotton. The shiny texture will reflect light and be far more prominent than the cotton cushion cover next to it, even though they may be exactly the same color.

Playing with texture and color combinations can have the most amazing effects. This is particularly important in monochromatic schemes. Here there are no big color contrasts to create the effect, and finishes become all-important.

Texture effects

◆ **Try to combine different textures** such as rough with smooth, shiny with dull, fluid with solid.

◆ **Depending on what effect you want** to create in your room, you may find it interesting to mix man-made finishes, such as highly polished metals, fake fur, and silky fabrics, to get a really contemporary feel.

◆ **In other rooms** you may want a very natural look with neutral colors and the interest coming from natural textures, such as leather, coir, and dull stone.

▶▲ Fabric finishes

Although these silk cushions are an almost identical color as the walls, they are a focal point because they are shiny and reflect more light.

▶ Talking textures

The interest in this room is produced by the textures of the natural materials of wood, brick, and plaster. The neutral colors allow the textures to tell the story.

▶▶ On reflection

In this room natural textures such as the carpet and the shades have been contrasted with the more reflective surfaces of the glossy walls and the metallic ceiling.

HOW COLOR WORKS

◆ **Sometimes you can mix the two** for an even more interesting effect. For example, a room full of neutral colors with natural-style textures can be transformed into something amazing by one polished metal accessory.

So how do you achieve those different textures and finishes in your rooms? Think of each section of your room and how you could use texture to enhance it. Try to think of each area in conjunction with the others.

Remember that the light in your room will change the appearance of the textures. A spotlight on a fabric will make it seem much shinier and make the color more dominant. Fluorescent light will reduce shadows and textures, so when you are thinking of each area, try to include the light sources in your decisions. Consider your wall coverings first as they are bound to be the largest expanse of color combined with texture. Then move on to your fabrics, floor coverings, and accessories.

Using texture effects

◆ **Paint manufacturers** have introduced many "novelty" products lately, such as glitter paints, metallic paints, paints with an iridescent swirl in them, chalky finish paints, and textured paints. This is in addition to the usual matte, silk, and glossy finishes.

◆ **Don't think you have to stick to paints** either. In the last couple of years, wallpaper has seen a big resurgence in popularity. You can buy most of the same finishes in wallpaper that you can with paints and once you've got the idea of hanging wallpaper, it's probably quicker than the painting option.

◆ **Don't forget the flooring** in your choices. Often left for last, this will also be a big expanse of color and finish, and it has a huge impact. Natural coir coverings will give a subtle effect, while polished linoleum in the same color will be considerably more vibrant.

▶ **Matte versus gloss**
Don't feel you have to paint all surfaces in the same finish. In this stunning space, the matte finishes on the walls and woodwork contrast beautifully with the shiny floorboards, black gloss paint detail, and the sculptural focal points.

EXPLORING
COLOR

warm

happy

calm

healing

vibrant

mysterious

relaxing

elegant

pure

sophisticated

COLOR PERSONALITIES: PRIMARIES

The final essential point to be made about color before you let yourself loose on your own color schemes, is the fact that each color has a "personality." A combination of inherited cultural influences and the way our eyes perceive color means that we attribute certain characteristics to it. These personalities can change across the world. For instance, purple is a grand, royal color in the Western world, but in Mexico it is a color associated with death.

Consider the primary colors first. Red, yellow, and blue in their purest forms all have different personalities, and they will have a subliminal effect in any color scheme. Their use will be saying things that you may or may not intend.

Primary color personalities

◆ **Red** is the color of danger, blood, and warmth and as such is pretty strong stuff. This is because it has a primeval association with fire and life itself in its positive and negative forms.

◆ **Yellow** is an easier color by far. Associated with sunshine and happiness, it can imbue a room with optimism and energy. If red means man-made warmth, yellow is natural warmth and light.

◆ **Blue** is present in our natural world in vast quantities—just think of the expanse of the sky and sea. As such, it is thought to represent the calmness of infinity and is seen as a healing color. Just as red represents warmth, blue can indicate coldness.

▶ **Cozy corner**

With its connotations of danger, red can be a fiery color to work with. But it also means warmth, and in this rather grand room it is used to create a cozier ambience.

▶▶ **Infinite calm**

Blue can be seen as cold, but it can also provide an aura of calm and, even in small measures, bring a feeling of the infinity of the sky or the sea.

COLOR PERSONALITIES: SECONDARIES

Secondary colors have their personalities as well, although they may be quite different from their neighbors, the primary colors. They each have two primary color parents, but the effect of mixing them produces quite different results.

Although the personalities of secondary colors may not be so strident as primary colors or have such a strong effect on you, they are definitely there. Like the more subtle human personalities in our lives, they are sometimes easier to live with. However, just like those people, it doesn't mean that these colors have weaker associations; you will still be creating a certain atmosphere by using secondary colors, so spare a little thought for what these could be.

Secondary color personalities

◆ **Orange** is a warm and stimulating color. Sitting between red and yellow on the color wheel, it draws from the attributes of both. A vital color, it is said to lift the spirits and be very sensual.

◆ **Violet** is a color of deep mystery and grandeur in its darker shades. Associated with pomp and circumstance for many, it also enjoys the paler personality of lilac and lavender, which represent meditation, healing and calm. Between the heat of red and the cool of blue on the color wheel, it will have a warmer personality the more red it has in its mix and a cooler one the more blue it has.

◆ **Green** is seen as a relaxing color. Actors rest in a "green room" between their exertions, and it is often thought to be an untaxing color. It is, of course, the predominant color of nature and sometimes seen as representing man's harmony with nature.

Green can also represent new beginnings in a world where green shoots are the beginning of a new cycle. Sitting between yellow and blue, it draws from both a warm and a cold parent. Consequently, the more blue a green has, the colder its personality will be and the more yellow, the warmer.

▲ **Energy boost**
Orange can be seen as a difficult color to use, but it is also supposed to lift the spirits, bringing an instant sense of vitality and energy.

▲ Perfect peace

Green is often thought of as very restful, and if it incorporates a good measure of genes from its yellow parent, it will be much warmer than if it has more from its blue parent.

◄ Calm oasis

The paler tints of violet imbue a room with a great feeling of calm and light, especially if they are combined with white. Add a little warm accent to bring zest to the room.

COLOR PERSONALITIES: NEUTRALS, BLACK & WHITE

It is easy to overlook that neutral colors also have a personality. The very word "neutral" seems to indicate an absence of emotional response. However, this couldn't be more wrong as neutral colors create a psychological reaction in us, although it may be more subtle.

Sometimes divided in different ways, "neutrals" for us can be interchanged with "naturals" and encompass browns, beiges, and creams. Our black and white include grays and all three groups of colors produce a quite different effect.

Neutrals and black-and-white color personalities

◆ **Neutrals** are the earth colors and as such have something of a primeval attraction for us. Sometimes misconstrued as dull and boring, they actually provoke a restful feeling in us, a feeling of security and solidity. They can induce feelings from serene elegance to rustic comfort. Creams add a touch of light and energy and are warmer than stark white.

◆ **Black** is often associated with oppression, evil, and death. On the surface, then, it would seem that it is not a very good color for interiors! However, it is also seen as sophisticated and its secret lies in association with other colors. A small amount of black can convey stylishness and elegance.

◆ **White** has connotations of purity and peace. Brides wear white and children have historically been dressed in white to symbolize their innocence. However, it can also symbolize an absence of emotion, a kind of stark and clinical void.

◆ **Gray** has some pretty negative connotations for us. Old age, "gray areas," and gray skies can be seen as fairly depressing. On the other hand, misty grays bring feelings of mystery and romance, while silver grays speak of elegance and value.

◆ **Black and white** is a combination that has a definite psychological response for us. The combination speaks of Art Deco and sophistication.

▶ **Subtle style**
Neutral colors have distinct color personalities, even though they are sometimes thought of as bland. Instead, they can bring particularly delicate hints of elegance and light to rooms.

▶▶ **Sophisticated set-up**
Black, white, and grays sound boring, but white brings a feeling of purity while black and grays speak of sophistication with just a touch of mystery.

ESTABLISHING COLOR FAVORITES

Different colors have different personalities, but that doesn't mean you have to react to them or use them in exactly that way. Orange may be vital and sensual, but you may hate it with a vengeance, no matter how vital and sensual you are!

How to . . . find your own color personality

◆ **Think of the colors you wear** and how they make you feel. Do you choose a yellow sweater to make you feel happier and more outgoing?

◆ **Maybe you have had** your colors analyzed by an expert, so will these work in your interiors?

◆ **Spread color cards** on your floor; to which general areas of color are you most attracted?

◆ **Think back over rooms** in which you have felt comfortable or uncomfortable or which have provoked a specific reaction in you. Was it because of the color, and what effect did it have on you?

◆ **Do you want your rooms** to have different personalities? Warm colors are often used in active rooms, such as kitchens, living rooms, and dining rooms, and cooler ones in restful rooms, such as bedrooms. This can never be more than a guide—there is nothing to stop you from having a blue kitchen. Use the key questions on page 42 to further help you establish your color favorites.

▶ **Bedroom bliss**
Subtle blues and whites can make for a particularly tranquil, airy ambience and are, therefore, ideal for a bedroom.

▲ **Vital energy**
If you feel energized by a scheme such as this, then the warmth and vitality of orange and yellow may be a good starting point for your scheme.

▲ **Going green**
Greens can be a good launchpad for choosing a bedroom color scheme, as they generally convey rest and relaxation.

EXPLORING COLOR

COLOR CONSIDERATIONS

1. What kind of atmosphere do you want to create in your room? For a relaxing atmosphere, try soft greens; for a cool, tranquil hideaway, take a look at blues; for a sharp and pristine appearance, black-and-white combinations can be especially chic; to de-stress, look to naturals and neutrals; but for cheering up, go with yellow; and for a convivial, cozy feeling, opt for deep reds.

2. What kind of natural light do you have in your room? If you have very little, choose a neutral color scheme; but if you must don the sunglasses when you enter, go with a soft green; for limited light, warm things up with sunny yellows; a good amount of warm, natural light means you can be liberal with blues; transform a room that receives nothing but cold light by using warm reds.

3. Which of the following descriptions best describes your personality? Sociable? Then convivial red could be for you. Glamorous? Opt for sophisticated black and white. Laid back? Go for relaxing green. Happy? Sunshine yellow may be your natural milieu. Dreamy? Soft violet could exactly suit your mood. Natural and calm? If this is the case, you may feel most at home with naturals and neutrals.

4. What will you be using your room for? If for food preparation and casual meals, yellow is a particularly cheerful color to choose; for something more formal, think black and white; in the bedroom, soft blues are safe; for communing with the natural world, greens will form a bridge between outside and in; for dining and entertaining, look toward muted reds; and, finally, for easy family living, you will find that neutral colors can form the perfect backdrop.

▲ **Grass green**

For a room that has a splendid view, use green to draw the outside in.

▲ **Cool white**

For a calm setting, a mainly white background will give you all the tranquility you need to relax.

▲ Hot housing

A red living room is for the more energetic among us—a convivial color, red does not encourage relaxation.

▲ Mellow yellow

Yellow is a cheerful and relaxing color that will always encourage you to wake up feeling happy.

▲ Bathed in blue

For a room that has plenty of natural light, blue walls will look fresh and envigorating.

▲ Naturally neutral

For family living, you can't go far wrong with a backdrop of neutral tones.

CREATING A
COLOR SCHEME

lifestyle

emotion

practicality

entertaining

lighting

architecture

springboard

swatchboard

testing

developing

CREATING A COLOR SCHEME

ROOM CONSIDERATIONS

Color may work in certain predictable ways, and as you know, each color has its own personality and suggests a different atmosphere, but a great deal will depend on your actual room and how you intend to use it.

Take time to really explore your room and try not to be too affected by colors and finishes that are already there but that you intend to remove. If you really can't get around these, remove the drapes and whitewash the walls and start with an empty canvas.

Remember that unless you live alone, you will have to consider the wishes, needs, and tastes of the other members of your family. This is the point at which you must really thrash it out as a group, if the room is going to be a success for everyone.

How to ... assess your room for color

Your first task is to identify how your room is going to be used. This will be a mixture of emotion and practicality so you can create a room that exudes the right atmosphere but is also realistic.

◆ **Living rooms** Do you use your living room for relaxing or entertaining, or a mixture of both? You may want to choose a warm color, such as yellow, peach, or pink, or a tranquil color, such as blue. If you feel that blue will be too cold, veer toward the warmer blues.

◆ **Dining rooms** These are often convivial rooms where you want to feel warm and friendly, so shades and tints of red are often popular. However, if you use your dining room mainly for breakfasts and lunches you may prefer a more inspiring color such as yellow.

◆ **Halls** This will give the initial impression to visitors to your house, so the color is really important. A relaxing, calm color, such as green, is popular.

▶ **Outdoor dining**

When decorating a dining room, consider the seasons you use it the most. This room is ideal for summer entertaining and the green-and-white scheme connects it to the garden outside.

◆ **Kitchens** Is your kitchen the heart of the house, or do you want it to be seen as a clean, hygienic food preparation area? If the former, veer toward the warmer terra-cottas, yellows, and peaches. The latter will lead you to whites, possibly teamed with cooler blues.

◆ **Bedrooms** These are often decorated in restful blues and greens for obvious reasons. Add a little warmth with soft pinks or warm violets.

◆ **Children's rooms** It's tempting to use primary colors but these can be too energizing for children, so primaries are often better confined to playrooms.

How to . . . make the most of your room

◆ **The architectural style** This may have a bearing on the colors you use in the room. If it is contemporary in style, you may use whichever colors are in fashion. But for a room with a distinctive period, why not research the colors that were used at that time?

◆ **The natural light sources** The sources of natural light in your room, that is, how much light comes in and the direction your room faces, will make a big difference to the way your color choice works.

◆ **Linking the room** Don't be tempted to think of your room in isolation. When the door is open, it will be linked to other rooms, so consider how the colors will work with other existing schemes.

◆ **Dividing the room** If you live in an open-plan area, you may want to "divide" the room by the use of color. Consider how you will accomplish this without it appearing too choppy.

▶ Architectural designs

A wealth of architectural features in this room has been emphasized by the use of subtle, period-style colors. Cream accents have been used to enhance all the period features, making the most of a very interesting room.

▲ Light fantastic
Natural warm light bathes this room, making it ideal for a neutral color scheme.

▲ Yellow duo
Warmth has been added to this high-ceilinged room with the use of two shades of yellow.

CREATING A COLOR SCHEME

SPRINGBOARD

What you really need now is a springboard for your color plans. It may be that the starting point has been handed to you or that you really have a clean slate, but you do need to consider the following.

How to ... make a start

◆ **You may have existing fabrics** that were just so costly you don't want to get rid of them. Or perhaps you love them so much that you have carried them from house to house.

◆ **Painted furniture** can always be changed, but you may adore it so much, it becomes your starting point.

◆ **Your room** may have a dominating architectural feature around which you feel all else has to revolve.

◆ **Find a color focal point.** It may be a rug, a large painting, or a quilt cover, but every room needs one.

◆ **Many color schemes** start from a much-loved vase, a pillow cover from a sale, or even the sight of a vase full of apple blossom. If this is your starting point, it is just as valid as a piece of furniture.

◆ **You may have the image of a room** you admire. It may be in a magazine, a great dwelling, or a friend's house. Try to get hold of a photo or the magazine page to keep your mind focused on the look.

▶▲ **Alcove elegance**
Centered around the elegant period alcove, this room cries out for a sophisticated and subtle color scheme, such as this beautifully muted apple green.

▶ **Fashion statement**
This color scheme is dominated by the existing, very strong marble floor design. The use of black and cream softens the whole scheme.

▶▶ **Strong statements**
A superb feature such as this "spider's web" window is so dominant that it combines beautifully with the truly strong colors of its surroundings.

MAKE A SWATCHBOARD

There is no need for you to try to keep all your color thoughts in your head. Create a swatchboard and you will have a visual record. Make it portable and you can use it to match colors, fabrics, and trimmings.

How to ... create a swatchboard

◆ **Obtain a large piece of** cardboard or corkboard that will not bend too easily.

◆ **Using pushpins, glue, or tape, affix swatches** of color, fabric, and wallpaper that feel right for your room—they are just ideas at this stage, so don't try for precision just yet.

◆ **Add any bits and pieces** that give the right color, texture, or effect. Dried flowers, sweets, trimmings, and even pieces of broken crockery can be attached.

◆ **Tear out pictures from magazines** or add some postcards. Besides pictures of interiors, look out for natural landscapes, pictures of cars, foreign scenes, and fashion plates.

◆ **Try to keep areas** of color to the right ratio. For instance, if you want your walls to be apple green and your cushions rose pink, have large pieces of green and smaller ones of pink on your swatchboard.

◆ **Don't paint colors straight** onto the card. Paint them onto another piece and attach them to the board in case you change your mind and want to remove them.

◆ **Be prepared to mix and match** and experiment. It may take some time to get the right combination.

▲ Collecting ideas

You don't have to use a board for your ideas—a journal can work just as well as a place to include fashion photos, pressed flowers, and trimmings.

◄ Swatchboard swamp

You can begin by covering your swatchboard with a whole collection of fabrics and ideas and gradually whittle it down as your scheme develops and your ideas change.

► Subtle differences

Experiment on your swatchboard with subtly differing tones and shades. This is the first stage of trying to get the ideal color that you can later test on the actual room.

TESTING & DEVELOPING

Once you are happy with your swatchboard, take it a step further and test your ideas in the actual room. If you haven't already allocated your different colors to their different places, approach your room by deciding on the largest blocks of color first, such as the walls, floors, and ceilings, then go on to the sofas, drapes, and rugs, and last, the accessories and smaller blocks of color.

Remember that basic color schemes should include no more than three principal colors, although additional colors can be added as accents. There is only one way to find out if a color scheme works for your room—test it.

How to ... test your color scheme

◆ **Paint large swatches** of color on the walls. Observe how the color can look dramatically different in various parts of the room and at different times of day.

◆ **If this doesn't produce** the effect you want, move up and down the tints and shades until you find the right one.

◆ **Hang a large piece of fabric** to represent your drapes. Try to buy a large enough piece to hang with folds as this will change the color. You can always use it for pillow covers later.

◆ **Fix large pieces of wallpaper** to the walls in different places and keep an eye on the effect at different times of day.

◆ **Try to test all the color combinations** you will be using. The combinations are just as important as the colors in isolation.

◆ **If possible, test your colors** under different artificial lighting conditions. You may be able to do this by using a light with a long cord and different types of lightbulbs.

▶ **Shifting shadows**
It is a very good idea to test your colors in several different parts of the room as they can look dramatically different depending on your natural and artificial light sources.

▲▲ Night and day

Because of the large amount of natural light in this room, it looks very different by day and night. Remember, it's very important to test your colors in both situations.

▲ Color surprise

The wall surrounding the fireplace looks much lighter than the window wall, even though they are painted in the same color. Remember this when testing your favorites.

COLOR
PALETTES

DETAILS MATTER

In all the assessing of your rooms and the careful decisions on your swatchboard, you have to look at color in considerable detail to make exactly the right choice.

Essentially, you will have to decide exactly how to use your chosen colors. You need to know which color is going to be dominant in your room and which you will use as accent colors. You need to consider whether you want a harmonizing or complementary scheme, and you need to look at all the tints and shades of your chosen colors before you make your final decision. For all of this, you have to know how each color works in all its glorious variations and how it combines with others.

In some ways, this is the most important and exciting part of the whole process because you are deciding precisely which colors to use and how to combine them. So with all the theory under your belt and your swatchboard at the ready, consider all your options and have fun.

► **Sultry decadence**
This wonderful sultry orange has been combined with a casbah-style theme to give an exotic and almost decadent passion to the room.

▼ **Color splash**
Here, a carefully neutral scheme has been lifted above the ordinary with the orange blocks of color for the pillows and throw.

NEUTRALS & NATURALS

ivory

cream

buttermilk

stone

taupe

ecru

sand

tan

chestnut

mahogany

FROM BEIGE TO CREAM

If you've opened any magazine on home interiors in the last few years, you can't fail to have noticed how popular neutrals and naturals have become in our homes. Different people mean different things by these terms but perhaps the easiest way to identify them is that neutrals are creams and beiges and naturals are ivories, sands, stones, and browns.

The reason these colors are so popular is that at the cream end of the spectrum they bounce light back into a room and make it seem airy without being too stark. At the brown end they are often warm and earthy and easy to live with. Remember, when you are using neutrals and naturals that as you are turning your back on bold color, there will be much more emphasis on shapes and textures, so give them extra thought.

▲ Understated charm
Neutrals are used to make this room seem airy without appearing too stark. A touch of interest is added by the crewelwork bedspread.

▶ Natural elegance
Neutrals can be a great choice for living rooms, especially if combined with the natural textures of stone, wood, wool, and basketwork, giving a very calm, sophisticated image.

TINTS & SHADES

Although you may feel that the neutrals and naturals of this world may not give you much scope, look at any paint chart or on the shelves of any paint store and you will be in for a very pleasant surprise. There has been a huge increase in the number of paint colors in the neutrals and naturals section and you will be spoiled for choice. There are many subtle gradations, but some good pointers are:

◆ If you are looking for a serene, yet sophisticated, look, you can't go astray with soft tones of cream or buttermilk combined with a smoky blue, or for a warmer effect, a soft terra-cotta.

◆ Or perhaps you are after a rustic look where you can combine some of the gutsier sand colors with russet and chestnut browns.

◆ Don't forget that much of your effect in these schemes could come from the shades and tints of wood, from the ethereal bleached ash to the stateliness of rosewood and mahogany.

◆ Although you may be loath to try it, combining pure white with pale naturals, such as stone, can look surprisingly effective.

◆ Remember that in the paler, very delicate schemes, anything you add of a stronger color will dominate the room, so be very careful with your accessories as they may stand out more than you intended.

▶▲ Dark touches

The tints and shades of neutrals can be easily "punctuated" with small amounts of dark wood and tiny dashes of black, especially in a very light and airy room such as this.

▶ Cream and chocolate

Here, neutrals and naturals have been employed from the palest cream to give the feeling of space and height, to the darkest chocolate to bring coziness.

TINTS ▷ 100% chestnut ▷ add white

▲ Creamy depths

You may think of cream as quite a limited color, but here several different shades have been used to great effect to bring interest and depth to this large living room.

◀ Light and dark

In this room the darker shades and the lighter tints of the neutral/natural range have been used in almost equal measure with very dramatic results.

SHADES ▷ **100% chestnut** ▷ **add black**

AS AN ACCENT COLOR

Many naturals and neutrals may be subtle and shy, but they can certainly pack a punch as accent colors.

In period interiors, neutrals are often used to highlight architectural details against a stronger color, such as Indian red or misty blue.

In minimalist white interiors, a range of neutrals and naturals, from stone through chestnut brown, can bring a much needed touch of warmth. If you want to get this effect, think of using a collection of pillows, each in a subtly different warm brown color.

Small touches of cream and buttermilk can lighten the effect of a room where the dominant color is perhaps just a little heavy-handed, but don't go for too much contrast or the effect will be too stark.

▲ Hidden depths
The very darkest shade of mole brown has been used in this warm yellow room to emphasize the large window and to add a little depth to the whole, otherwise less daring, scheme.

▲ Showing it off
This beautiful bed has been thrown into greater relief by the contrast with the very palest of neutrals and white. The linen and soft furnishings only serve to offset the ornate wood carvings of the bed frame.

▶ Pretty purity
Combine accents of buttermilk with virginal white for the creamiest, prettiest effect. The textures in this room are quite sumptuous, too—enjoy the combination of rough-hewn walls, complex carvings, and softest wool.

NEUTRALS & NATURALS

MODERN STYLE

If you want to create a really contemporary interior, look no further than neutrals and naturals. These colors have become the easy-to-live-with basis of a look that relies on natural materials for its beauty. But it's sophistication that's the name of the game, not rusticity. Colors range from creams and taupes to glowing nut brown. Keep decorative detail to an absolute minimum, relying instead on blocks of natural color and the inclusion of different textures.

The absence of bright colors means that shape is very important and softly curving, organic shapes look really wonderful against this backdrop. The end result should be airy, comfortable, and subtly sensuous.

▲ Organic naturals

Understated neutrals and naturals are ideal partners to the organic shapes and natural materials—all that wood in different forms—that are often used to their best effect in contemporary schemes.

Unassuming shades and tints of natural colors give this room an undemanding aura and make it feel incredibly light and airy.

Organic, curving shapes add to the comfortable, natural atmosphere of the whole scheme.

Different textures are thrown into relief against the subtle, natural hues of the gentle color scheme.

◀ **Naturally calm**

A range of neutral colors has been used in this Modern-style room to emphasize the impression of space and light.

YELLOW TO ORANGE

sunshine

buttercup

gold

lemon

primrose

ocher

apricot

tangerine

rust

terra-cotta

FROM LEMON TO GOLD

Close your eyes and conjure up the color yellow. What do you see? Most people will visualize the yellow of buttercups, sunshine, or egg yolks. Yellow as a primary color is warm and strong, and as such lends a cheerful, optimistic feeling to a room. A very welcoming color, it can make large spaces seem smaller and more intimate. However, too much really bright yellow in the wrong room could send you reaching for the shades, so be a little discriminating.

Of course, the really bright, primary yellow is only part of the story, as yellow can range from the almost-cream buttermilk, through yellow green. Whichever tint or shade you choose, they will all add a varying amount of warmth, which makes it a favorite color for many rooms.

▲ **Instant cheer**
Yellow can do wonders for warming up a large room and brings instant cheeriness to north-facing rooms, which tend to be a little gloomy.

▲ Yellow glow

Egg yolk yellow has been used with plenty of white and black in this room to give a warm, but not overpowering, glow throughout that is never overdone.

◄ Spring herald

Various shades of yellow have been cleverly combined here to give a spring-like freshness to this living room. In such a large, light room, a liberal use of intense yellow would have been over-powering. Here it has been limited to the sofa and lampshade.

FROM LEMON TO GOLD 73

YELLOW TO ORANGE

TINTS & SHADES

From creamy buttermilk to deep gold through all the warm sunshine yellows and the more challenging acid hues, the different shades and tints associated with yellow can bring quite different effects to your interiors. Before you choose, consider the following:

◆ Straight-between-the-eyes egg yolk yellow will instantly bring an uplifting sense of sunshine, but be careful not to overdo it.

◆ A lighter tint of primrose will have a gentler, more delicate effect, which you might find easier to live with.

◆ Lemon yellow brings a more "acid" touch, which is striking when used in the right room.

◆ Yellow ocher is a duller yellow that looks wonderful in older-style properties and more ethnic interiors.

Oranges as tints and shades

Tell friends you're painting your walls orange and they may recoil, but if you consider the gentler tints and shades, orange becomes a different proposition. Look back at the color wheel (see page 16) and you will see there are oranges, red-oranges and yellow-oranges, all of which give varying amounts of warmth or brightness.

◆ Apricot is an easy color to live with, blending well with blues, greens, and grays.

◆ In the red/orange arena, rusty orange is rich and warm without being too arresting.

▶▲ Soft buttermilk
A buttermilk wall coloring gives a wonderfully warm and peaceful aura to this room. Mix it with palest cream and off-white and it becomes fresh and spring-like.

▶ Adding mustard
Wide stripes of yellow and mustard give a depth of color in a room that might have seemed just slightly dull had it been painted in just a single color.

TINTS ▷ 100% yellow ▷ add white

▲ Piquant pair

An acid yellow tint adds a certain piquancy to this room, especially when mixed with egg yolk yellow.

▲ Inspired work

In this office, a burnt umber shade has been teamed with a sunshiny yellow to combine inspiration and cheerfulness, creating a perfect working environment.

▶ Sunny solution

In this striking room, primary yellow sits alongside a deep shade of orange and a brown-orange, making the stronger primary yellow the focal point of the room.

SHADES ▷ 100% yellow ▷ add black

AS AN ACCENT COLOR

If your room needs a little zing to lift it above the ordinary, a touch of yellow or orange can certainly do the job. Just think of the way a vase of daffodils or a bowl of oranges can instantly bring sunshine and warmth to a room and you will feel the power of yellow and orange as accent colors.

Adding splashes of yellow will bring an uplifting glow to the dullest interior, while touches of orange can bring either small focus pools of warmth, or a certain edge, a feeling of living just a little dangerously.

Remember that yellow can make a more interesting contrast for deep colors than white, working well with deep blues and greens and contrasting with crimson for a striking effect. Refer to your color wheel (see page 16) to get the optimum combinations, but don't be afraid to play around with different shades and tints (see page 18).

One final word—don't forget the power of gold as an accent color. There's no doubt that a touch of gold can transform a simple scheme into something much grander, but it does have to be handled with great care. The trick is to add the color with a frugal hand and to remember that shiny gold will be far more dominating than a matte finish.

▲ **Yellow connection**
Different tints and shades of yellow have been used in this space as accent points, partly to relieve a fairly dark brown but also to lead the eye from one room through the magnificent hallway.

◀ **Sunshine drops**
Bright white often benefits from a few yellow accents, as they introduce a warmth and metaphorical touch of sunshine to an otherwise somewhat sterile room.

▲ Sunshine flood

Sometimes it's just right to revel in a huge dollop of sunshine yellow. Here, a buttercup yellow wall serves as an accent to bring the otherwise more neutral color scheme into sharp focus.

◀ Orange glow

In a room that focuses on a neutral palette, the orange chair pads introduce a touch of warmth to the room.

YELLOW TO ORANGE

COMPLEMENTARY COLORS

One quick glance at the color wheel will tell you what the marriage made in heaven is for yellow and orange. In terms of contrast, blues and violets are the perfect partners for them. Strictly speaking, violets are the best contrast for yellows, and blues for oranges. The reason for this is that each combination is a sublime mix of just the right amount of warmth and coolness, but don't get too hung up on it—it's a starting point.

Getting complementary

◆ Yellow-oranges look best with blue-violets.

◆ Combine yellow-greens with red-violets.

◆ Red-oranges look vibrant with blue-greens.

It does depend on what effect you are trying to achieve. For instance, a slightly acid yellow is on the cooler side of the yellow spectrum and will become gentler when mixed with a deep warm blue, but if you don't want to make it gentler, mix it with a cooler blue.

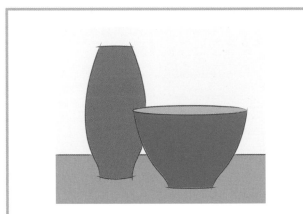

Blues and violets are perfect partners for shades of yellow and orange. For a warm combination, choose from the violet end of the spectrum. If you want to tone down a hot orange, look to the cooler blues.

▶ Mysterious passion

Misty, romantic lavender has been partnered with vibrant primary yellow for a balanced effect. The room would be much brasher without the calming pale violet tones.

▲ Perfect bedfellows

Warm orange and cooler mid-blue make good bedfellows with their complementary hot and cold attributes. Dashes of burnt orange and hot pink have been added to bring a little interest.

HARMONIZING COLORS

If the contrasting or complementary colors for yellow and orange all come from the opposite and cooler side of the color wheel, the harmonizing colors will obviously all come from the warmer side. These will be schemes where the overall look is warm and easy, with nothing to challenge the eye too much. For any color, its immediate neighbors on the color wheel will provide the most obvious combinations. However, don't be afraid of straying a little further around the wheel. As long as you stay on the "warm" side of the wheel, the colors should harmonize beautifully.

The perfect combinations:

◆ A combination of buttercup and soft orange will bring instant, sunny warmth.

◆ Acid yellow with pistachio green introduces a sense of "edge" to a room.

◆ Terra-cottas and deep reds give a sensuous, cozy atmosphere.

◆ Tangerine, soft yellow, and mulberry can be sharp and warm all at the same time.

However, don't be afraid to look a little further than the immediate neighbors. A certain and even more interesting harmony can be obtained by combining, say, a yellow-orange with a red-orange or a yellow with a red-orange, even though they are not directly next to each other on the color wheel.

▶▲ Sweet harmony

Candy stripes of harmonizing red, yellow, and pink may seem a very bold combination, but here they combine brilliantly, working together to give a general effect of warmth and light.

▶▶ Fresh start

Irresistible in its freshness, this refreshing color scheme successfully mixes sunshine yellow with a more restrained spring green. The end result most definitely makes your heart sing.

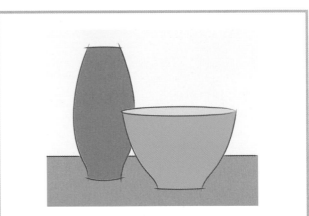

For a dash of complementary pairings, try teaming yellows and oranges with other warmer colors, such as yellow-greens for a fresh effect, or reds and pinks for a little added heat.

YELLOW TO ORANGE

CARIBBEAN STYLE

Think of the Caribbean and you'll think of jewel colors and dazzling light. One thing this look is not, is subtle. If you want to get the Caribbean feel in your room, bathe the whole area in sunshine yellow, and then add generous amounts of vibrant turquoise, hibiscus pink, and emerald green. If you can't face such a dazzling scheme, tone it down by using shades and tints of these colors, but keeping to the basic principle.

This isn't the whole story though. To get the classic Caribbean look, think of elegant verandas with white-painted furniture and shutters, and light, airy rooms with fans.

▲ Flower power

Dramatic splashes of color rather than intricate patterns work best with the Caribbean look. If you want to introduce florals, make them big and bold, but don't overdo it as the vibrant colors will make a big impact.

This yellow is a gentler tint than the one on the adjacent wall. But it still fills the room with the feeling of sunshine without too much dazzle.

Blocks of strong color bring the vibrant Caribbean landscape to this room, while leaving the airy, light-filled effect to dominate.

White-painted shutters are reminiscent of the elegant plantation houses, and they also make for a much lighter touch than drapes.

Dramatic house plants bring the feeling of lush vegetation.

There's no fussiness in this big, bold floral pattern which suggests the colorful flowers of the Caribbean.

◀ **Paradise colors**

This room instantly says Caribbean as it cleverly brings together all the essential elements of that style, such as jewel colors, bright florals, lush vegetation, elegant shutters, planters, and chandeliers.

SPANISH STYLE

The Spanish look is influenced by the hot, dry climate and local materials. Add to this the exotic influences of the Moorish style and you have a distinctive and exciting look. Colors are derived from the terra-cottas and burnt umbers of the local earth and the warm yellows of sunshine. Splendid turquoises, vivid greens, and warm pinks combined with Moorish gold can all be added as accent colors.

Combine wrought iron and dark wood with whitewashed adobe walls to give a sensuous yet rustic look. Keep this look relatively basic, but comfortable. Think of lengthy siestas hiding away from the burning sun, surrounded by the colors of the natural landscape, when it's just too hot to go out there.

▲ **Moor luxury**

Go ahead and create the excitement of Moorish luxury by teaming rich orange with some gloriously vibrant pinks, purples, and greens.

Dark, rustic wood beams add depth to the whole interior, also helping to bring a high ceiling a little closer.

Warm terra-cottas have been used to give this interior the necessary earthy look of the Spanish style.

A simple, small touch of accent color stands out as a focus contrast to the rest of the room.

Terra-cotta floor tiles strike a truly authentic note, but these have been chosen with plenty of warm yellow as well as orange.

◀ **Spanish siesta**

A simpler Spanish look is achieved here with plain terra-cotta, whitewashed walls, and earthy colors. Splashes of brighter orange and yellow tell of the heat outside.

RED TO PINK

plum

burgundy

tomato

rose

shell

raspberry

mulberry

vermilion

cherry

lipstick

RED TO PINK

FROM ROSE TO PLUM

From full-blown, danger sign red through delicate shell pink, reds and pinks denote either passion or romance. Whichever shade or tint you choose, rest assured they will definitely bring a visual and emotional warmth to your rooms, whether it be bright and vivid or reserved and gentle.

All the primary colors have to be used with care, but red is probably the least suited for use as a dominant color, because it is so strong. However, take it just a couple of shades or tints in either direction, and it can work beautifully.

There are the very bright pinks that work best for outgoing personalities or in a child's bedroom. For instant sophistication, go for the more subtle shades and tints, or for the romantic look, use delicate hues.

▲ Warm welcome
Maybe you have a cold, north-facing room that needs warming up, or a living room that could really benefit from the instant coziness of a deep red.

▶ Convivial dining
Red may seem a little overbearing, but here it has been served up with generous dollops of cream and white to counter some of the heat.

▲▲ Smart stripes

Reds and deep pinks can be very smart used as stripes and particularly when matched with white.

▲ In the pink

Pink and off-white is the perfect bedroom combination; same color combinations but different patterns introduce variety.

TINTS & SHADES

It's no accident that we call so many of the reds and pinks by edible or potable names. There's something about our reaction to this spectrum of colors that makes us want to indulge, whether it be in the earthy, full-blooded pleasures of the burgundies and clarets, or the more delicate attractions of crushed raspberry and cotton candy.

◆ **Plums and burgundies:** the deep, bluish reds give a feeling of warmth and security, and, therefore, are a great choice for dining rooms and living rooms.

◆ **Indian reds, terra-cottas and russets** are soft versions of the primary color, and while they still bring that lovely feeling of warmth, they are just so much easier to live with.

◆ **Pale pink** has a great deal of white in its composition which makes it a very fresh, pretty color.

◆ **Hot pinks** certainly make a statement but are still more comfortable than primary red. Remember, they can bring enormous impact even in small amounts.

◆ Muted pinks, such as raspberry and mulberry, are some of the easiest colors to get along with.

▶▲ Indian caramel

There is just enough caramel in this room of Indian red to make the unusual pairing with a sophisticated silver gray extremely successful.

▶ Soft terra-cotta

A pinky terra-cotta is used with soft verdigris for a very unusual color scheme, but one that is both warm and soft on the eye.

▶▶ Berry cocktail

Here, hot pink has been used with the more calming influences of crushed raspberry and mulberry, imbuing the whole room with a sensuous warmth.

TINTS ▷ 100% red ▷ add white

RED TO PINK

AS AN ACCENT COLOR

If you are looking to add a touch of instant focus to your room, nothing will speak louder than a strong red or pink scattered around the space. Because reds and dark pinks are very domineering colors, just one item in these shades can immediately transform a room. The difficulty lies in avoiding excess. Less is certainly more in this case.

Add a dash of tomato red and you are immediately adding a smart touch. Like a woman dressed in black with bright red lipstick, you will be achieving instant chic. By the same token, hot pinks and shocking pinks can work very well as accent colors. Slightly softer than the primary red, they are still chock full of impact and work brilliantly with soft blues and greens.

But don't run away with the idea that pale pinks are too wishy-washy as an accent. In a very pale room, they can bring that touch of warmth that transforms a neutral scheme and makes it look less stark.

▶ **In the pink**
The warmth of this wonderful old rug is echoed in small touches around the room, such as pillows, photographs, and a section of the painting above the chair.

▼ **Hot stuff**
Even one hot pink accent will instantly rivet the eye in an otherwise delicately white room.

COMPLEMENTARY COLORS

A quick glance at our trusty color wheel (see page 16) will reveal that the most obvious complementary color for reds is green. There is something particularly satisfying about this combination and the thought of raspberry pink and emerald green is tantalizing indeed. But there are some other wonderful combinations to consider as well.

Getting complementary

◆ **Olive green and Indian red** have a similar saturation and can be used in equal amounts as they don't fight with one another.

◆ **Tomato red and cool turquoise green** are stunning together, although a little goes a long way.

◆ **Primary reds, vermilions, and scarlets** work very well with other vivid colors, such as yellow and bright yellow/green.

◆ **Combine cherry and claret** (the cooler reds) with gold for a deeply satisfying look. Somehow, the hotter reds look cheap with gold.

◆ **Red and white** are a very popular combination seen particularly in gingham, checks, and stripes. The combination of warmth and coolness gives a very crisp effect.

◆ **Soft pink and powder blue** form a marriage made in heaven, giving a soft, dreamy effect.

You can successfully combine reds and pinks with blues and greens in a variety of complementary mixes, bringing together hot and cold to enhance one another. The results can be quite arresting.

◀ **Color equals**

Soft olive and Indian red are made to complement each other. Neither are too hot nor too cold, and because they have the same intensity, they can be used in equal measures.

▶ **Dramatic duo**

Drama has been added to this room by pairing bold tomato red with a complementary cool lapis lazuli blue. The effect is sensational.

HARMONIZING COLORS

If you are looking for a warm but relaxed combination for reds and pinks, raid the stronger colors of the "hot" side of the color wheel. These are very strong and can be vivid when combined with their complementary colors, but when mixed with harmonizing neighbors, even the hottest colors become relaxing and more easygoing.

In perfect harmony

◆ **Combinations of** even quite hot reds and pinks actually work really well together.

◆ **A marriage of salmon pink** and tangerine may sound odd, but can look surprisingly good.

◆ **Even deep mulberry** and touches of scarlet can live together successfully.

◆ **If you are looking** for something a bit different, hot pink and buttercup yellow are both from the "warm" side of the wheel and make a wonderfully strong statement together.

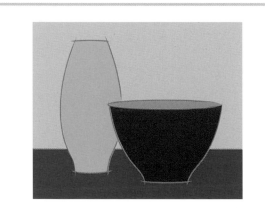

It may sound a little racy to combine reds and pinks with oranges, yellows, and mauve, but, in fact, they work together with incredible success as they are adjacent, harmonizing colors.

▶ **Brash comfort**

Deep, satisfying plum can be given a saucy embellishment with a little tomato red. At right, a little frivolity saves the room from becoming too ponderous.

▲ **In perfect harmony**
Crushed mulberry and
salmon terra-cotta are
used together here in
another, rather surprising
but wholly successful,
harmonizing combination.

◀ **Classical grandeur**
If you want a rather grand
effect reminiscent of the
Byzantines, go for a
combination of deep
burgundy and egg yolk
yellow, as here.

FOLK ART STYLE

Folk Art is a very popular naïve style developed by settlers who wanted to lift their homes above the basic, to bring warmth and simple design to them. They used the natural pigments that were available and their homemade designs were strong and striking, as befitted the pioneer spirit of the time.

Earthy pink-reds and red-oranges were great favorites and were often teamed with greeny-blues and olive greens. This was offset with a widespread use of cream so that rooms didn't appear too dark. To achieve the look, be bold. It may have been simple, but colors and designs were strong, often incorporating themes from the natural world or patriotic designs for a new country.

▲ Homespun comfort
What could be more homespun and cozier than this red-and-yellow kitchen? It oozes warmth, comfort, and good, old-fashioned family times.

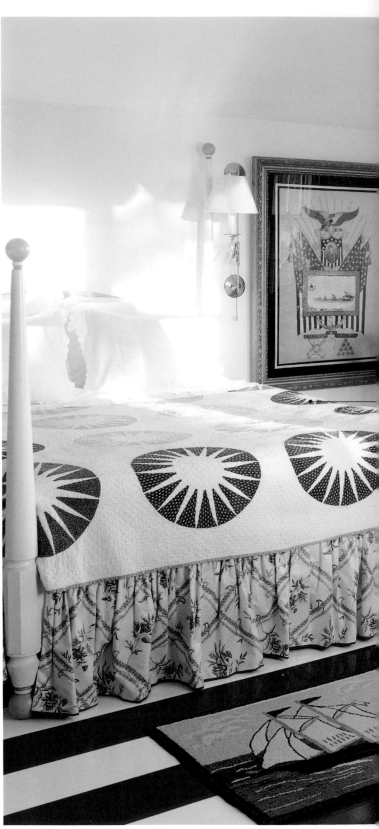

Strong designs in striking contrasting colors are used to give instant impact. This is the confident look of pioneers building a brand new world.

Cream and off-white are used to offset the strong colors and patterns and to bring light into the room.

Intricate patchwork designs can incorporate many colors, but for maximum effect, use vividly contrasting shades.

Patriotic designs are also popular, using the same bold, warm reds.

◀ **Patriotic folk**

Patchwork is an integral part of the Folk Art style, and the bold pattern on this quilt tries to dominate the room almost as much as the flag-waving red-and-white striped floor. Here, bold red has been used to reinforce the décor's patriotic theme.

ENGLISH COUNTRY STYLE

If you want pure romance, go for the English Country look. Start by thinking of a very old, quiet English rose garden and you're halfway there. Colors here are muted, with shell and rose pink dominating. Mix these with apple and mint greens and touches of deep, soft pink and warm lavender for a very peaceful look.

In terms of pattern, florals are a definite must and the more delicate and intricate the better. Uncomplicated designs, such as checks and stripes in muted colors, are all part of the look, but don't be too strident.

Simple painted furniture in pale tints such as cream, lichen, and shell pink work well with stripped wooden floorboards or natural fiber floorcoverings and intricately patterned rugs. Walls can be washed in the same muted color palette, or in simple cream.

▼ Pretty in pink

It's hard to think of a more romantic room than this pretty English garden style. A mix of delicate patterns, all in the same colorways, is matched with subtle gingham and stripes.

Pale lichen greens are used to give a restful effect and gently combine with the shell pinks.

Shell pink is a signature of this look and can be brought into focus with touches of darker rose pink.

Gentle florals bring intricate pattern and Old World charm to this room. A certain amount of warmth and focus are introduced by using a deeper pink, but make sure these accents do not overwhelm the delicate scheme.

Creamy lace completes the picture, but never overdo it; one simple piece is often enough.

◄ **Country dreaming**

The dreamy effect in this room has been achieved by bringing together the prettiest of rose and shell-pink florals and fabrics with hints of pale apple, mint, and Wedgwood blue.

BLUE TO VIOLET

azure

lavender

lilac

aqua

amethyst

teal

powder

cobalt

lapis

delft

FROM AZURE TO LILAC

The color of the sea and the sky (on a good day!), blue is all around us in the natural world and is also a very popular color for interiors. Blues for your rooms do have to be chosen with care, though. Because they inhabit the cooler side of the color wheel, they can make a room seem uninviting to the point of iciness. Much will depend on your room. If you have a north-facing room, you may be better off opting for a warmer blue to take the chill off. But blues can also bring with them a feeling of airiness and of liberating space, a stimulating feeling of the infinity of outdoors.

Take a step or two from primary blue toward the heat of red on the color wheel and you have the violet family. The few degrees of extra warmth introduces the soft clarity of lavender through lilac, which speaks not so much of wide-open spaces, but of gentleness and sensuality. These colors may not be so liberating, but they are often easier to live with and work better in rooms where you want to relax.

▲ Seating plan
Lapis blue chairs add a stimulating dynamism to this dining room, bringing excitement to what would otherwise be a far more pedestrian space.

▲ Formal entertaining
Bordering on deep turquoise, this blue dining room has been combined with white to give a formal rather than convivial atmosphere.

▲ Grand reflections
Strong cobalt blue is a brave choice that works well in this living room, especially as it has been highlighted with a highly ornate mirror feature.

▲ Clean cut

Pale blue can sometimes seem too icy in north-facing rooms, but where the light is right, it can be clean and fresh.

◄▲ Cool contemporary

This strong blue combined with white is perfect for a very contemporary room that is flooded with warm, south-facing light.

◄ Lovely lilac

Shades of lilac have been successfully combined in this relaxing feminine living room. There is sufficient white woodwork to prevent the color from creating a cloying atmosphere.

TINTS & SHADES

From dapper navy blue through all the more forgiving cornflowers and hyacinths, blue can definitely be a color chameleon in your room schemes. For instance:

◆ **Misty blues** with just a hint of gray immediately speak of romantic Scandinavian landscapes and look wonderful washed over woodwork.

◆ **A touch of green** in the blue to produce pale aqua brings that feeling of cleanliness so ideal for bathrooms.

◆ **Slightly warmer, lighter blues**, such as azure or powder blue, can instantly call to mind days on the beach and seaside joys, which is a wonderful effect to capture in your rooms, especially for the winter months.

Violet as tints and shades

With their extra degree of warmth, the violet tints and shades create a quite different effect than blue:

◆ **Deep purple** is a very royal color that will bring instant formality to a room.

◆ **Add another little bit** of red warmth and the result will be the far more forgiving and cozier shades of plum and violet blue.

◆ **Add some more red** and you are in the realm of glowing amethyst.

◆ **The paler tints of lavender** and lilac introduce some femininity and delicate prettiness to a room, a look that is ideal for bedrooms.

▶ **Delft dream**
Delft blue, almost bordering on the violet, has a hint of warmth that saves this room from appearing horribly cold and clinical.

TINTS ▷ 100% blue ▷ add white

▲▲ The Old World
Here, a combination of gray-blues gives an overall Old World effect.

▲ Soft touches
Pale blue and soft violet have been used together with a sparing hand, giving this living room a gentle, informal setting.

SHADES ▷ **100% blue** ▷ **add black**

AS AN ACCENT COLOR

If you want to add an instantly elegant and fresh look to a predominantly white room, nothing works better than a clear blue. One vase or one striped shade with just a touch of blue will transform the room and give it that feeling of freshness.

Touches of bright blue give an uplifting vibrancy to a pale yellow room, a kind of "edge" that focuses the whole scheme and lifts it way above the ordinary. Be careful not to overuse this color, though, as it can all too easily dominate and drown the quieter yellow.

You can also have great fun using violet as an accent color. If you suddenly crave a splash of sophistication and a certain regal touch, add some glowing amethyst and maybe a touch of dull gold to your rich cream or ivory interior.

Or maybe you want to go to the other, more fanciful, end of the spectrum. Nothing is more subtle, or speaks more of fresh delicacy than a hint of lilac or lavender with crisp white. White fabrics scattered with pale lilac flowers are almost unbearably pretty and you can always focus the whole image with one lilac satin lampshade.

▶ **Attention grabber**
This fabulous pair of rich blue vases are reflected in the mirror for extra accent impact. The art of accent placement is not difficult to learn—be as bold as you like.

▲ **Cobalt focus**
One intensely cobalt blue vase in this neutral color scheme immediately lifts the room above the ordinary.

▲ **Subtle point**
Soft medium violet can be used as an accent in a room where you don't want the accent to dominate too much.

COMPLEMENTARY COLORS

The natural complementary colors for blues and violets are oranges and yellows, but you can draw from the whole of the warmer side of the color wheel for a wide range of effects. As a general guide, think of combining your cooler blues with warmer yellows and oranges and the warmer the violet, the more you can afford a little coolness in the yellow.

Getting complementary

◆ **Deep, warm shades of blue** go well with the cooler yellows, but also with plaster pink.

◆ **Pale gold** and a lighter tint of blue with just a hint of gray can look very sophisticated.

◆ **The cooler shades of blue,** such as duck egg, need something a little warmer, such as russet or apricot, to bring them alive.

◆ **Deep or mid-violet** and pale primrose can be just stunning when combined.

◆ **Powder blue** and pastel pink is an example of a slightly warmer blue and a slightly cooler pink working well together.

◆ **Raspberry and teal** also look wonderful when sitting together in the same room.

▲ **Natural match**
The tan-colored wood and the natural fiber rug in this room add just enough of an orange hue to bring out the best in the various blues without making the contrast appear stark. With their harmonizing hues, the carefully positioned purple pillows on the chaise longue help to give balance to the overall finish.

▶ **Restraining influences**
Gray-blue and gold is a cool and sophisticated combination that speaks of restraint and elegant living.

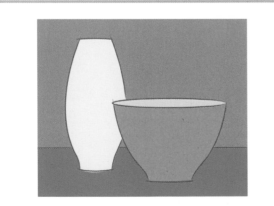

Yellows and oranges are the perfect complementary bedfellows for all shades and tints of blue and violet. Whatever combination you choose to use them in will give a deeply satisfying result.

BLUE TO VIOLET

HARMONIZING COLORS

If you are looking for calm and serene combinations for blue and violet, choose from among their harmonizing colors. These are, of course, predominantly greens and turquoises. The closer together colors are on the color wheel, the more harmony there will be, but sometimes you need to look a little further. Remember that combining blue with the red violets will make it look warmer and combining it with greens will make the same blue look cooler. The success of your harmonies here could depend on the quality of light in the room.

In perfect harmony

◆ **The old maxim** that blue and green should never be seen doesn't have to be followed, but mid-blues and mid-greens probably work best together. Try emerald and cobalt for a rich effect.

◆ **Blue-greens and violets** are far enough apart to produce a cooler and warmer combination that works well. Pale lilac and pale gray-blue can definitely learn to live together.

◆ **Combine tones** of blue and violet for a restful effect, and if it looks too dull, throw in tiny splashes of white, yellow, or another pale color.

▲ **Quieter friends**
Even quite a stark blue-and-white combination, such as this rug, can harmonize well with gentler mauves.

◀▼ **Genteel dining**
Different tints and shades of blues, violets, mauves, and deep pink are combined on this wooden dining table in a charming mode.

▶ **Working together**
Mauves and bright blues are combined in this room to enhance one another. The bright blue lifts the room from heaviness, while the mulberry tones down the slight brashness of the blue.

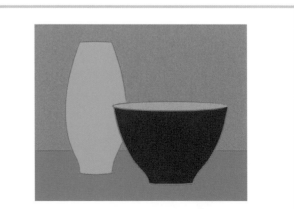

For a room that is dominated by blues and/or violets, look to the harmonizing colors in the mauve and aqua-green spectrum of the color wheel when seeking some comforting color combinations.

SWEDISH STYLE

Taking its cue from the muted tones of the natural Scandinavian landscape, the Swedish look draws from misty blues, blue-greens, creams, and grays. This gives elegant, restful rooms, often focused with a simple touch of accent cherry red or scarlet.

Wooden furniture is the order of the day, either left in its natural pale state or painted and distressed. The pieces are often designed with graceful organic curves. Rooms should be light-filled but not cold.

The look can be either rural Scandinavian or the more elegant Gustavian style of the wealthy with its tiny touches of gilt and draped fabrics. These fabrics are often plain, but checks are very popular, too.

▲ **Dreamy blues**
Swedish style quite often takes the softest of muted blues and teams them with gray, cream, or white and then adds a flash of blood red. The flowers on the corner table are a successful example, although the effect could have been achieved just as easily with a small painting.

"Distressed" painted furniture in pale colors gives the impression of age and longevity, which increases the peaceful feeling in the room.

Cream, such as the color used on the painted floorboards, has been used throughout this room to reflect light and make the room seem airy. The absence of drapes improves the light.

Muted gray-blues have been used on various pieces of furniture to give that truly restful Swedish look.

Painted furniture with organic curves is typical of the Swedish room, bringing a touch of elegance to a very rustic look.

◀ **Be natural**

A color palette of muted blue-grays and creams is teamed with painted wood and gentle shapes in a lovely and quintessentially Swedish setting.

GREEN TO
TURQUOISE

pistachio

jade

lime

sage

moss

emerald

apple

olive

avocado

lichen

GREEN TO TURQUOISE

FROM LIME TO SAGE

Green is generally thought of as being a very relaxing color, putting us back in touch with Mother Nature and being very easy on the eye. In many cases this is true, but introduce some of the yellow-greens into your rooms and you will create immediate excitement. As dominant colors these can be amazing, if sometimes a little too exhilarating. Muted greens also work well as a dominant color but will probably need splashes of something more brilliant to bring them into their own.

Turquoise is a color closely associated with green. Think of the luscious turquoise stone and you will understand why the color has been prized throughout history. A combination of blue and green, it can be a very dominant color in its darker shades. Toward the paler end of the spectrum it becomes aqua and is very popular in bathrooms for its lovely, watery effect.

▲ Spring green
This intensely pretty, soft jade green is used as a backdrop to floral paintings, ribbon bows, and painted furniture for a soft, gentle atmosphere.

◄ Dream catcher
Soft lichen green gives a dream-like, relaxing quality to this room, which is then enlivened by touches of turquoise.

◄◄ Green splash
Green may be seen as a relaxing color, but here yellow-green is used in all its vibrancy to create a striking room.

TINTS & SHADES

From the deep, somber green of evergreens, through the gray-greens of sage and moss and the yellow-greens of apple and pistachio, green is versatile enough for you to use in every room in your house if you choose to! Don't overlook the power of:

◆ **Emerald**, which is surely one of the strongest and most satisfying greens. If you feel too inhibited to use it as a dominant color, it makes a great accent.

◆ **Deeper bottle greens**, which give a fabulously "period" feel to a room, especially in a matte finish.

◆ **Light moss greens**, which combine a welcoming air with a feeling of relaxation, are a fabulous choice for hallways.

◆ **Apple greens**, which can bring a very "happy" feeling to a room.

Turquoises as tints and shades

Turquoises or blue-greens range from the deep teals through to the mints, saying very different things about a room. Bright turquoise is gorgeous, but quite hard to use in interiors. However, if you have your heart set on it, don't back off, just make sure you do all your testing thoroughly! Or consider some alternatives:

◆ The **deeper teals and jades** are an unusual choice but can work beautifully; just be careful not to go too dark and somber.

◆ At the other end of the spectrum you have the **minty greens**, which give a fantastically fresh and sparkling feeling to a room, making them an obvious choice for bathrooms and powder rooms.

▶ **Aqua revival**
Turquoise bordering on aqua has been used in soft enough tints in this room so that it seems reviving rather than too intense.

▲ **Upwardly mobile**
Soft jade has been used here in an unusual way, matching stairs to walls. Making such a feature of the stairs makes one want to climb up to see what mysteries lie beyond.

▶ **Easy-going green**
This light moss green must be one of the easiest colors to live with, somehow managing to be both relaxing and welcoming at the same time.

TINTS ▷ 100% green ▷ add white

GREEN TO TURQUOISE

AS AN ACCENT COLOR

Add a hint of green to your room, especially a brighter yellow-green, and you will bring immediate spring freshness to your interior. Combine this with ivories, deep and pale pinks and you have instant apple blossom.

Other greens also work really well as accent colors. If you want your room to take on a rich feeling, opt for an emerald green. You may feel this color is just too much of a good thing as a dominant color, but there is nothing to stop you reveling in it as an accent. Even the more muted greens, such as sage, work well as accent colors, toning down bright pinks and bringing a subtler tone to your room.

A touch of turquoise can also lift a color scheme. The brighter the turquoise, the less you need, but it can be very dramatic even in these small doses. If you are thinking of adding a very bright turquoise to a bright yellow scheme, do proceed carefully, as the second bright color can make the first look cheap, but add a slightly muted turquoise to straw and you have a very special combination, and a touch of teal with raspberry is simply mouthwatering.

▶▲ Fresh lime
A mouthwatering lime-green accent is perfect for this very fresh, airy room, making it look almost good enough to eat. The green has been picked up in the tub of ferns and casual flower arrangement on either side.

▶ Jade focus
Just one small area painted in intense jade will be a focal point for any room. Here the small cupboard door is balanced by a tall vase containing colored flowers from the opposite side of the color wheel but of the same intensity.

▶▶ A gentler touch
The touches of green in this yellow room—a tiny glass lampshade, seats on chairs, even a hint at the back of the cupboard—soften the whole effect and make it an easier room in which to relax.

COMPLEMENTARY COLORS

Examine any garden and you will see just how well green contrasts with myriad colors. The color wheel shows us that its natural complementary colors are reds, but there are some wonderful other complementary combinations.

Getting complementary

◆ Tomato red and emerald green may be just too much for an interior, but go for a little more subtlety and look at the rich combination of jade and terra-cotta.

◆ **Equally delicious** is the combination of olive green and burnt orange, bringing warmth and rest in equal measures.

◆ **Apple greens and amethysts** make natural partners, providing a mixture of rich glow and freshness.

◆ **If you are looking for** a muted but deeply satisfying effect, consider the combination of sage and either pale powder pink or apricot.

◆ Just as apple green and white can be stunning when used together, so can mint and white, giving that squeaky clean effect.

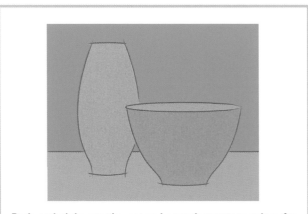

Reds and pinks are the natural complementary colors for greens and turquoises. But try out some oranges, too—just slightly removed from red on the color wheel—as you will find they work extremely well.

▶ **Lime and lavender**
Vibrant pistachio green will bring freshness and life to a muted lavender scheme. Use the far more dominant green with care as it can easily overpower the shier violet tints.

▲ **Apricot dream**

Moss green and soft red are a very satisfying complementary combination, especially when combined with white.

◄ **Orange twist**

Combine soft avocado green with touches of the brightest orange for an unusual look.

HARMONIZING COLORS

You may think that a combination of blues and greens could be very dull, and you would be right, it can be. But certain combinations are surprisingly effective, depending on the mix of warmth and coldness in the colors.

In perfect harmony

◆ Choose a vibrant apple green and team it with cool teal and you will have an unusual combination.

◆ Put a drab olive green with a buttercup yellow and you will have a successful combination used again and again in the natural world.

◆ The slightly warmer tones of jade can combine well with royal blue, but test combinations of tints and shades before making your final decision.

◆ Moving slightly further around the cool side of the color wheel, blue violets such as lavender combined with turquoise can be very satisfying for a room that needs a calm aura with just a slight edge.

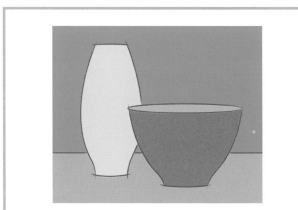

Forget the old maxim that "blue and green should never be seen." Choose the right shades of each color and they can work perfectly together. Turquoise also combines well with violets and green with yellow.

▶ Traditional calm

Soft, silvery green has been used in this room with an equally soft, creamy yellow to liven it up, without totally removing the relaxing effect the green brings.

▲▲ Blue yonder

In this room a dull olive has been paired with a warmer blue and then highlighted with a floral splash of yellow.

▲ Citrus splash

Sunshine yellow and lime green can work together as long as one doesn't dominate the other. This might work best in a slightly dull room, as it could be too bright in a room that is filled with natural light.

FEDERAL STYLE

To reproduce the Federal style, think grand. Based on the elegant European Regency and Empire styles, this style also owes something to a confident new America at the start of the nineteenth century.

This confidence is reflected in the bold colors used in the era. Vibrant greens and dusty pinks are teamed with old gold and lightened with cream and muted plaster pink for the details. Duck-egg blue and pale gold are another elegant combination for formal rooms.

Grand, Classical architectural features are the order of the day, often painted in a paler color such as cream or white to throw them into relief against the stronger, dominant colors of the room.

▲ **Total impact**
If you are lucky enough to have an impressive feature like this grand, Classical doorway, it can look even more amazing if it is picked out in white or cream against a darker color, such as this leaf green.

Pale gold and duck-egg blue are used here for a very elegant, formal look, reflecting the growing confidence of a new nation.

Classical moldings recall ancient times and provide a feeling of history and solidity for the citizens of a newly emerging power. They also call attention to the wonderful proportions of the room.

Touches of old gold in lamps, frames, curtain rods, and on furniture lend the room a certain restrained grandeur.

Wide Regency stripes are used as the only pattern and dominate the room, increasing the formal atmosphere but not appearing brash.

◄ **Refined styling**

A pale gold-and-green scheme has here been mixed with elegant gold and duck-egg blue to create the most sophisticated of color schemes for a room whose proportions are a testament to timeless grace.

BLACK &
WHITE

slate

dove

jet

ebony

charcoal

silver

pearl

snow

alabaster

platinum

FROM JET BLACK TO SNOW WHITE

There are few people who are brave enough to choose black as a dominant color for a room, but many who will opt for white. Like the paler neutrals which reflect light so well, white will make your rooms appear airy and spacious, but beware it doesn't become too stark and unwelcoming. Avoid this overly clinical look by choosing a slightly warmer white.

On the other hand, if you are looking for something undeniably sophisticated and chic, a black-and-white mix can be stunning. This combination will introduce a level of formality to a room, which is the reason that it is often used in hallways and formal rooms but not so often in bedrooms. However, there is nothing to stop you! The effect may just be a little easier on the eye though, if you go easy on the black and introduce a warmer light source or a touch of buttermilk, taupe or sand to take the edge off.

▼ Pure and simple
White is the predominant color in this bedroom, but organic shapes, soft fabrics, and a touch of ecru prevent the room from looking too stark.

▲ **Practical living**
A black-and-white combination can look spiffy and clean in a very masculine-style bathroom.

▲ **Paint it black**
Using black as a predominant color requires both good design sense and a certain bravado, but it works in this paneled room full of strong images and designs.

▶ **Textural combinations**
The different textures of washed floorboards, plaster, and wood have been enhanced by the slightly differing shades of white in this hallway.

BLACK & WHITE

TINTS & SHADES

In theory, there are no such things as tints and shades of black and white, hence the expression of something being black and white with no gray areas! But consider the subtleties:

◆ Gray, of course, is a tint and a shade of both black and white.

◆ There are also many, many whites. These will probably be pure white mixed with various other colors, but they will still be termed white, because they have such infinitesimal amounts of color in them.

◆ Obviously, a white with a hint of blue will give a misty effect, while one that has a hardly discernable drop or two of red or yellow will instantly make your room look warmer.

◆ The same happens with grays. Think of the softness of dove gray compared to unforgiving iron gray.

◆ Then there is the lovely dull slate and the gentle blue-grays so associated with Swedish interiors. Thinking of gray as dull and boring is a dangerous thing to do when it comes to decorating!

▶▲ Bringing peace
Soft dove gray has been used to make this light-filled room seem bathed in gentle shadows. The high proportion of blue in the gray is relaxing and meditative.

▶ Backing it up
The gentle grays and taupes in this room serve as a neutral backdrop to the interest of the cushion design and the painting on the wall.

▶▶ Dream on
Silver gray has been used to wonderful effect in this room, giving it an unhurried, almost dreamy quality. Hints of soft green and orange add a little contrast, but don't leap out at the viewer.

TINTS ▷ 100% black ▷ add white　　　　**add black ◁ 100% white ◁ SHADES**

the best reve

AS AN ACCENT

It is surprising what a difference a touch of black or white can bring to a room. Use both judiciously as they will rivet the eye in certain interiors.

If you are using white, the stronger the color it is teamed with, the more the white details will appear as a highlight. This can be a great use of white as an accent, to highlight a feature, or draw attention to that general area. For instance, a small row of white pots will make you notice the subtle decoration of the shelf they sit on.

Using black as an accent color can have even more dramatic effect. In a white or neutral interior, even a black photo frame will seem to leap out in stark relief. Obviously, in stronger-colored rooms the effect will not be so great, but it will definitely make its presence felt, so use with care and don't overdo it, or your interiors could look too dark and imposing.

▲ **Small pointers**
A masterpiece of understatement, this arrangement uses small white bowls as an accent to attract the eye to the beautiful plasterwork below them.

▲ Sharpening up

In the room above, black has been used as an accent to bring the red color scheme into sharp relief and give it a very handsome appearance. Note that the drapes are diaphanous rather than opaque, which could have been too overbearing.

◀ Black magic

A little black can go a long way as the use of this framed mirror shows in a mainly neutral room. Be careful you don't overdo black when you're using it as an accent color, as it tends to take over a room.

BLACK & WHITE

COLONIAL STYLE

As the name suggests, early colonists brought this look, which is broadly based on the English Georgian style. To reproduce the same atmosphere, concentrate on simple yet elegant solidity. This is a look that has little embellishment or fuss, just lovely structure.

Dark woods taken from local forests were combined with a very limited palette of colors. Often this was white or cream, or muted natural pigments, such as China yellow and soft blue-gray.

It is important to keep decoration simple in this overall scheme. Enliven the plain soft furnishings and polished dark woods with only the tiniest of accent touches of muted color and pattern.

▲ Simple contrast

When used well, black and white make a wonderful color scheme for the Colonial look because of its very simplicity. In this room the trunk has been echoed by curtain poles and pictures as well as some furniture, but the touch is light.

Whitewashed walls make this room seem incredibly airy and pure, speaking of the serenity of a quieter, simpler age.

The elegant lines of this beautiful bed are enhanced by the simplicity of the room and the dark, almost black wood against the whitewash of the rest of the decoration.

The very limited decoration is largely provided by the intricate designs on the pillows and chair.

Tiny touches of accent color, such as these pink-and-white flowers, are all that is needed in this quiet color scheme.

◀ **Old charm**

The quietness of a simpler and slower age is reflected in this black-and-white color scheme. Only the tiniest hint of color is allowed in the small posy of flowers, and a sense of airy peacefulness is maintained.

COLOR
SOLUTIONS

COLOR ENHANCES PROPORTION

Let's face it, there's no such thing as the perfect dwelling. All houses and apartments have problem areas or spaces that could be improved, and sometimes expensive building work is required. Not always though. Before you go down that route, remember that there are few rooms that the clever use of color cannot help. Through color, you can create optical illusions that make your rooms look larger, smaller, higher, and wider.

It all goes back to how colors work, especially their receding and advancing properties. If you walk into a room and the wall facing you is painted red, it will seem closer than if it were painted pale blue. This is because red is an advancing color, making objects appear nearer, and pale blue is a receding color. Generally speaking, warm, dark colors advance, and pale, cooler colors recede. If you are in any doubt, paint a cardboard box and place it at the end of a corridor and see whether it advances or recedes from you.

▶ **Super stripes**
A tent-like paint effect has seemingly brought a high ceiling lower in this room, making it more intimate.

▼ **Warming up**
This vast room is made cozier by painting the far wall in an advancing warm yellow, making it seem closer and so rendering the living space less cavernous.

MAKING SMALL ROOMS APPEAR LARGER

At some point in their decorating careers, most people will need to make a small room look larger. Don't be daunted by small rooms, as amazing things can be done with the right colors.

The first thing to remember is to keep it simple. Too many colors or too much pattern will make the room appear cramped. Keeping in mind the fact that certain colors advance on you and make objects appear closer, avoid strong colors such as deep reds and emerald greens.

Instead, opt for soft, paler colors as they reflect light and recede to give the illusion of a larger room. Neutrals and naturals are a great choice and the warmer, paler grays are surprisingly space-enhancing.

Make the most of the natural light sources in the room, keeping the drapes pale. It's best to use harmonious colors for the walls and drapes or shades rather than contrasting colors that will divide the limited expanse of wall.

◀ **Making space**

This small dining area has been made to look larger by using the same color on the ceiling and walls and a very similar one on the door and floors. This means there are fewer breaks and distractions for the eye and the whole space seems more cohesive.

▲ **Parallel lines**

If you want to make a room look wider, bold horizontal stripes can work wonders. Use them vertically, and the room would have looked taller. Notice too, that the floorboards have been laid running in the same direction to enhance the whole optical illusion.

MAKING HIGH CEILINGS APPEAR LOWER

Many of us dream of the luxury of high ceilings but they can bring their own problems. In some houses, large, grand rooms may have been split up to make smaller rooms, leaving the space totally out of proportion. Whatever the reason, if your ceilings are too high, any atmosphere of coziness or intimacy will be destroyed.

If this is the case, don't panic! Don't rush to put in false ceilings as the canny use of color will be just as effective and much less expensive. If you use a darker color on your ceiling, especially an advancing one such as warm nut brown, it will immediately give the effect of the ceiling appearing nearer.

This can be achieved by either painted or stained wooden cladding, but a far easier and cheaper solution is to use a color that is a slightly darker than the vertical walls. If you use a harmonious color, the effect will be more subtle than a contrasting color; but a contrasting color can make the ceiling a feature in its own right.

Don't forget that you can enhance this effect by also using a warm, advancing color on the floor as well, bringing ceiling and floor instantly closer together.

▲ Lower company
Painting your ceiling in a warm, advancing color such as red can make it seem closer and, consequently, render the whole room cozier.

◀ Sly stripes
High ceilings may seem to be a blessing, but in some rooms they can be a burden. Painting horizontal stripes that encroach slightly on the ceiling tie the ceiling and the wall closer together and give the illusion of the ceiling being nearer.

▶ Getting closer
This high vaulted ceiling could have made the room look just too cavernous. Instead, it seems to have been lowered by painting it black.

MAKING LOW CEILINGS APPEAR HIGHER

If you are afflicted with low ceilings, you will know just how small and depressing they can make a room look. This is a difficult problem to overcome as there is really nothing you can physically do to make the ceilings higher. What you can do, however, is be clever with your color choice and use.

Just as you bring a high ceiling down by using a darker, advancing color, you can "raise" a ceiling by painting it a lighter, more receding color than the walls.

Or you can paint the walls and the ceiling the same receding color and make it one big expanse, giving a more spacious feel.

Another trick you can use is to utilize the power of stripes. Just as vertical stripes can make a small person look taller and thinner, they can make a room walk taller, too. If you think stripes sound a bit dramatic, remember that they can be very subtle, harmonizing colors and still create the right effect.

▲ **Stealing height**
In this room the light color on the ceiling has been brought about a foot down the walls, seemingly adding more height to the room.

▲ **Raising the roof**
Rooms with low ceilings can appear oppressive, so "raise" the roof by painting the ceiling a paler color than the walls.

◄ Bringing it together

This room is charming for children but does have a very low-pitched ceiling. This has been addressed by painting it the same pale color as the walls.

▼ Beam me up

With the wooden beams left exposed, this ceiling could easily have become overbearing. But the white paint reflects light, making the ceiling appear higher than it actually is, and it beautifully offsets the natural properties of the surrounding wood.

MAKING NARROW SPACES APPEAR WIDER

Long, narrow rooms can be very difficult to deal with. Not only are you faced with the problems of furnishing them, but they can feel like very uncomfortable spaces.

If you think of a narrow space as being too long for its width, the obvious remedy is to "bring" the far end of the room closer. By using a darker color, such as terracotta or mulberry, you can make the end of the room appear closer, and so the room's length seems more in proportion with the width, giving a wider appearance.

Another option is to press stripes into service once more. Just as vertical stripes will make a room seem higher, horizontal stripes will make it appear wider. However, be careful here. The best place to put the stripes is on the wall facing you when you walk into the room. This will instantly make the room seem wider. If you put horizontal stripes on the side walls, you could be in danger of making the room look even longer, which is the very opposite effect you're aiming for.

▶ **Mirror magic**
Mirrors have been cleverly used in this bathroom to reflect a darker color from the other end of the room and thus foreshorten the corridor-like space.

▶▶ **Broadening horizons**
This glorious wood paneling looks good but also serves an important aesthetic purpose. In a long, thin room, it brings the end wall closer and seems to even up the proportions of an awkward space.

COPING WITH CORRIDORS

As a general rule, corridors can be quite difficult to cope with. Designed as a means of getting from A to B, corridors can be unloved by their owners. This is a big mistake, as pampered with a little of the right color, they can be a big asset.

By their very nature, corridors are often narrow, so just like long, narrow rooms, you can transform them by making the end seem nearer. The difference is that in long, narrow rooms, the end point will be a wall, whereas in a corridor it is more likely to be a wall and a door, or an opening.

If this is the case, try painting the door or both the door and the wall an advancing color. If you can see through an opening into another room, why not make sure that room is painted in an advancing color?

In addition, the walls of the corridor will look wider if they are painted in a pale, receding color, and you paint the ceiling the same color. You could also place a few brightly colored paintings or objects along the walls at irregular intervals, so your eye is drawn in a kind of zigzag motion, rather than straight down the "tunnel."

▶ Warm reflections

Shiny, reflective floors and pools of warm light have been used in this awkward corridor space to create maximum visual interest.

◀ Diamonds are forever

One of the problems with corridors is that they are often fairly tiny places. Here, a diamond pattern has been used on the floor to give the illusion of a far bigger area than just the space under the stairs.

◀◀ Light fantastic

Paint an entrance hall a sunny, welcoming color and you will have all your visitors jumping with joy, whatever its size.

DIVIDING SPACE WITH COLOR

If your living space, or part of your living space, is open plan, you may face a dilemma. How can you divide it aesthetically without putting in physical barriers, which defeats the object of a wonderful open living area? The answer is, divide it with color. Harmonizing colors are sometimes the easier choice and live together happily, even if you do have several different areas and hues. Try different shades and tints of the same color spectrum. For a more dramatic effect, use stronger, contrasting colors.

Don't forget the opportunities that pattern and color together can give you. Again, you can go for the peaceful look of using a solid color and a pattern in the same or harmonizing color. Alternatively, a strong pattern and a different vibrant color can work and give the effect of two completely different rooms. The secret is to make sure one doesn't dominate the other and make that area of the living space more important.

▶ **Natural selection**
This large, open space has all been painted in one color apart from the dining area, which is delineated as a separate living space by painting the walls in a soft olive green.

▼ **Deep divisions**
Here, the open-plan living space has been divided in a dramatic way. The physical divider is only Plexiglas, but the aesthetic divide is all provided through the use of color.

UNIFYING SPACE WITH COLOR

Every house or apartment has areas that are potentially awkward and they can tend to look "chopped up" if not drawn together. Maybe you have a dominant stairwell that needs to take a cohesive design from front door to bedroom level, or a small open-plan area you want to connect with another living space to make it look bigger.

Color can be vital in these situations, but think carefully before you choose as this color has to be the perfect middleman. In the case of stairwells, the color has to be right for two floors and fit with all other décor when the doors are left open. It can't be too dominant a color because there will be so much of it.

If you are trying to unify rooms that lead into one another, using the same colors in both will throw them together. While color on the walls is important, floor coverings and furnishings can do the trick just as well.

▲ **Joining it up**
This kitchen has been included in the larger living space of this home by running the same wall color between the two.

◀ **Big and bold**
Stairwells are notoriously difficult because the colors used have to suit all floors. Here, a dramatic unifying effect has been achieved with the striking black-and-white combination.

▲ Connections

The entrance hall in this house is a beautiful space in its own right, and it has been connected with the other levels by using a creamy color throughout.

◄ Joint venture

With the exception of the carpets the furnishings don't match in these adjoining rooms. But the color scheme does and so the rooms are successfully pulled together.

PHOTOGRAPHY CREDITS

The publisher would like to thank the following photographers for supplying the pictures in this book:

Page 1 Carlos Domenech; **2** Antoine Bootz; **3** Jonn Coolidge; **4 top** Toshi Otsuki; **4 bottom** Edmund Barr; **5 top** Jonn Coolidge; **5 bottom** Carlos Domenech; **6** Luca Trovato; **8** Alexandre Bailhache; **9** Roger Davies; **10** Carlos Domenech; **11** Scott Frances; **12 left** Tim Beddow; **12 right** Fernando Bengoechea; **13** Gordon Beall; **14** Roger Davies; **15 top** Jacques Dirand; **15 bottom** Jeff McNamara; **17 top** Roger Davies; **17 bottom left** Luca Trovato; **17 bottom right** Guy Bouchet; **18** Jonn Coolidge; **19** Jacques Dirand; **21** Grey Crawford; **22 left** Jonn Coolidge; **22 right** Hugh Stewart; **23** Dana Gallagher; **24 top** Eric Roth; **24 bottom** Eric Roth; **25** Tim Beddow; **26 left** Simon Upton; **26 right** 1342 Studio; **27** Susan Gentry McWhinney; **28 top** Guy Bouchet; **28 bottom** Lizzie Himmel; **29** Fernando Bengoechea; **31** Oberto Gili; **32** Colleen Duffley; **33 top** Luke White; **33 bottom** Tria Giovan; **34** Michel Arnaud; **35** Jeff McNamara; **36** Dana Gallagher; **37 top** Jacques Dirand; **37 bottom** Jeff McNamara; **38** Pierre Chanteau; **39** William Waldron; **40 left** Gordon Beall; **40 right** Oberto Gili; **41** William Waldron; **42 top** Erik Kvalsvik; **42 bottom** William Waldron; **43 top left** David Montgomery; **43 top right** Guy Bouchet; **43 bottom left** Elizabeth Zeschin; **43 bottom right** Dominique Vorillon; **44** Tim Street-Porter; **44 top** Antoine Bootz; **44 bottom** Carlos Emilio; **47** Gridley & Graves; **48 left** Oberto Gili; **48 right** Tim Street-Porter; **49** Peter Woloszynski; **50 top** Peter Margonelli; **50 bottom** Colleen Duffley; **51** Tria Giovan; **52** Toshi Otsuki; **53 top** Toshi Otsuki; **53 bottom** Toshi Otsuki; **54** Thibault Jeanson; **55 top** Laura Resen; **55 bottom** Michael James O'Brien; **56** Dominique Vorillon; **57** Guy Bouchet; **58** Richard Bryant/Arcaid; **59** Jacques Dirand; **60** Eric Piasecki; **61 top** Valerio Mezanotti; **61 bottom** Fernando Bengoechea; **62** Pieter Estersohn; **63** Francis Amiand; **64 top** Tria Giovan; **64 bottom** Laura Resen; **65 top** Pieter Estersohn; **65 bottom** Jacques Dirand; **66 left** Tim Street-Porter; **66 right** Christopher Drake; **67** Jeff McNamara; **68** Tria Giovan; **69** Peter Margonelli; **70** 1342 Studio; **71 top** Maura McEvoy; **71 bottom** Scott Frances; **72 left** Gordon Beall; **72 right** Scott Frances; **73 right** Alec Hemer; **74 top** Guy Bouchet; **74 bottom** Guy Bouchet; **75 left** Grey Crawford; **75 top right** Bruce Buck; **75 bottom right** Oberto Gili; **76 left** Fernando Bengoechea; **76 right** Jonn Coolidge; **77 top** Courtesy of *House Beautiful*; **77 bottom** John M. Hall; **78** Jonn Coolidge; **79** Victoria Pearson; **80** Toshi Otsuki; **81** Jonn Coolidge; **82** Jonn Coolidge; **83** Gordon Beall; **84** Eric Roth; **85** Dominique Vorillon; **86** David Montgomery; **87 top** Tim Street-Porter; **87 bottom** Oberto Gili; **88 left** Roger Davies; **88 right** Jeff McNamara; **89 top right** Edmund Barr; **89 bottom right** Carlos Domenech; **90 top** Christophe Dugied; **90 bottom** Tim Street-Porter; **91** Fernando Bengoechea; **92** Guy Bouchet; **93** Victoria Pearson; **94** Jonn Coolidge; **95** Fernando Bengoechea; **96** Curtis Taylor; **97 top** Guy Bouchet; **97 bottom** Oberto Gili; **98** Tom McWilliam; **99** Jeff McNamara; **100** Antoine Bootz; **101** Susie Cushner; **102** Christophe Dugied; **103 top** Scott Frances; **103 bottom** Gloria Nichol; **104 left** Jonn Coolidge; **104 top right** Pieter Estersohn; **104 bottom right** Luca Trovato; **105 top left** Simon Upton; **105 top right** Steve Freihon; **105 bottom** Dana Gallagher; **106** Elizabeth Zeschin; **107 top** Oberto Gili; **107 bottom** Eric Boman; **108 left** Tom McWilliam; **108 right** Christopher Drake; **109** Jonn Coolidge; **110** Simon McBride; **111** Tria Giovan; **112 left** Melanie Acevedo; **112 right** Jonn Coolidge; **113** Minh + Wass; **114** Staffan Johansson; **115** Simon Upton; **116** Erik Kvalsvik; **117 top** Thibault Jeanson; **117 bottom** Roger Davies; **118 left** Jonn Coolidge; **118 right** René Stoeltie; **119** Colleen Duffley; **120 top** Christopher Drake; **120 bottom** Chirstopher Drake; **121** Jonn Coolidge; **122 top** Jonn Coolidge; **122 bottom** Roger Davies; **123** Barbara and René Stoeltie; **124** Jeff McNamara; **125 top** Erica Lennard; **125 bottom** Tim Street-Porter; **126** Alexandre Bailhache; **127 top** William Waldron; **127 bottom** Eric Roth; **128** Richard Felber; **129** Tim Street-Porter; **130** Eric Piasecki; **131 top** Jonn Coolidge; **131 bottom** William Waldron; **132** William Waldron; **133 left** Fernando Bengoechea; **133 top** Tom Crane; **133 bottom** Jeff McNamara; **134 top** Pieter Estersohn; **134 bottom** Fernando Bengoechea; **135** Polly Eltes; **136 left** Jeff McNamara; **136 right** Alec Hemer; **137** Pieter Estersohn; **138** William Waldron; **139** William Waldron; **140** Jeff McNamara; **141** Jonn Coolidge; **142** Courtesy of *House Beautiful*; **143** Jeremy Samuleson; **144** Roger Davies; **145** Tom McWilliam; **146 bottom** Fernando Bengoechea; **146 top** Gordon Beall; **147** Grey Crawford; **148 left** Gordon Beall; **148 right** Eric Piasecki; **149 top** William Waldron; **149 bottom** Susan Gilmore; **150** Fritz von der Schulenburg; **151** Tom McWilliam; **152 left** Simon Upton; **152 right** Polly Eltes; **153** Scott Frances; **154** Oberto Gili; **155** Thibault Jeanson; **156 left** Victoria Pearson; **156 right** Matthew Milman; **157 top** Peter Aaron/Esto; **157 bottom** Fernando Bengoechea.

INDEX